The Essential Guide to Internet of Things (IoT)

Engineer's Essentials

Published by Engineer's Essentials, 2024.

THE ESSENTIAL GUIDE TO INTERNET OF THINGS (IOT)

First edition. August 3, 2024.

ISBN: 979-8224256907

Written by Engineer's Essentials.

Table of Contents

Chapter 1: Introduction to IoT

Introduction

Welcome to "The Essential Guide to IoT: Building Smart Systems with Arduino and Beyond." The Internet of Things (IoT) is revolutionizing the way we interact with the world around us. From smart homes and cities to industrial automation and healthcare, IoT applications are transforming various industries. This book aims to provide you with a comprehensive understanding of IoT, from the basic concepts to advanced applications, with practical examples and hands-on projects.

What is IoT?

The Internet of Things (IoT) refers to the interconnected network of physical devices embedded with sensors, software, and other technologies to collect and exchange data with other devices and systems over the internet. These devices range from everyday household items to sophisticated industrial tools. The goal of IoT is to extend the power of the internet beyond computers and smartphones to a whole range of other things, processes, and environments.

History and Evolution of IoT

The concept of connected devices has been around since the 1980s, but the term "Internet of Things" was coined by Kevin Ashton in 1999 during his work at Procter & Gamble. Ashton envisioned a system where the internet is connected to the physical world via ubiquitous sensors.

Key Milestones in IoT Evolution:

- **1982**: The first internet-connected appliance, a Coke machine at Carnegie Mellon University, was able to report its inventory and whether newly loaded drinks were cold.

- **1999**: Kevin Ashton coins the term "Internet of Things."

- **2008**: The number of connected devices surpasses the number of people on the planet.

- **2014**: Major advancements in smart home devices, such as the Nest Learning Thermostat, gain popularity.

Key Components of IoT Systems

IoT systems are composed of several key components that work together to achieve connectivity, data collection, and intelligent decision-making.

Sensors and Actuators: Sensors collect data from the environment, such as temperature, humidity, motion, and light. Actuators perform actions based on the data received, such as turning on a light or adjusting a thermostat.

Connectivity: Connectivity refers to the communication protocols and networks that connect devices and enable data exchange. Common communication protocols include Wi-Fi, Bluetooth, Zigbee, LoRa, and cellular networks.

Data Processing: Data collected by sensors is processed either locally on the device (edge computing) or sent to the cloud for processing. Data processing involves filtering, analyzing, and deriving meaningful insights from raw data.

User Interface: The user interface includes applications and dashboards that allow users to interact with IoT devices and visualize data. This can be in the form of mobile apps, web interfaces, or voice commands.

Applications of IoT in Various Industries

IoT has a wide range of applications across different industries, enhancing efficiency, convenience, and safety.

Smart Homes: IoT enables home automation systems that control lighting, heating, security, and entertainment systems remotely. Examples include smart thermostats, security cameras, and smart speakers.

Healthcare: IoT devices in healthcare enable remote monitoring of patients, collecting vital signs, and managing chronic diseases. Wearable devices such as fitness trackers and smartwatches monitor health metrics and provide real-time data to healthcare providers.

Industrial Automation: IoT is transforming manufacturing processes through predictive maintenance, asset tracking, and real-time monitoring of production lines. This leads to increased efficiency, reduced downtime, and cost savings.

Agriculture: IoT applications in agriculture include precision farming, where sensors monitor soil moisture, weather conditions, and crop health. This data helps farmers make informed decisions about irrigation, fertilization, and pest control.

Smart Cities: IoT enables the development of smart cities with efficient energy management, intelligent transportation systems, and enhanced public safety. Examples include smart streetlights, traffic management systems, and waste management solutions.

Retail: IoT in retail enhances the shopping experience through smart shelves, inventory management, and personalized promotions. RFID tags and beacons help track inventory and analyze customer behavior.

Energy Management: IoT applications in energy management include smart grids, which optimize energy distribution, and smart meters that monitor energy consumption in real-time.

Summary

This chapter provided an introduction to the Internet of Things, covering its definition, history, key components, and applications. IoT is a transformative technology that extends the power of the internet to a vast array of devices, enabling smarter interactions with the physical world. As we move forward, we will delve deeper into the architecture of IoT systems, the hardware and software required, and practical projects to help you build your own IoT solutions.

Keep Going!

You're on your way to becoming an IoT expert! In the next chapter, we will explore the architecture of IoT systems, laying the foundation for building smart and interconnected devices.

Chapter 2: IoT Architecture
Introduction

In this chapter, we will explore the architecture of IoT systems, laying the foundation for building smart and interconnected devices. Understanding the architecture is crucial for designing efficient and scalable IoT solutions. We will discuss the key components of IoT architecture, including sensors, connectivity, data processing, and user interfaces.

IoT Network Architecture

The architecture of an IoT system can be broken down into several layers, each serving a specific function. These layers work together to collect, process, and transmit data, enabling intelligent decision-making.

1. Perception Layer

- **Sensors and Actuators**: The perception layer includes sensors that collect data from the environment (e.g., temperature, humidity, motion) and actuators that perform actions based on this data (e.g., turning on a light, adjusting a thermostat).

- **Examples**: Temperature sensors, motion detectors, light sensors, humidity sensors, relays, motors.

2. Connectivity Layer

- **Communication Protocols**: This layer is responsible for transmitting data from the sensors to the next layer. It includes various communication protocols such as Wi-Fi, Bluetooth, Zigbee, LoRa, and cellular networks.

- **Examples**: ESP8266 Wi-Fi module, Bluetooth modules, Zigbee transceivers, LoRa modules.

3. Edge Computing Layer

- **Local Data Processing**: Edge computing involves processing data locally on the device or at a nearby gateway, reducing latency and bandwidth usage. This layer can perform initial data filtering, aggregation, and analysis.

- **Examples**: Arduino boards, Raspberry Pi, edge gateways.

4. Data Processing Layer

- **Cloud Computing**: This layer includes cloud platforms that provide extensive data storage, processing, and analysis capabilities. It enables large-scale data analytics and machine learning applications.

- **Examples**: AWS IoT, Microsoft Azure IoT, Google Cloud IoT.

5. Application Layer

- **User Interfaces and Applications**: The application layer provides the user interface and applications that allow users to interact with the IoT system, visualize data, and control devices.

- **Examples**: Mobile apps, web dashboards, voice assistants.

IoT System Design Principles

Designing an effective IoT system requires careful consideration of several principles:

1. Scalability

- Ensure that the system can handle an increasing number of devices and data volume without compromising performance.

2. Interoperability

- Design the system to work with various devices, communication protocols, and platforms, enabling seamless integration and data exchange.

3. Security

- Implement robust security measures to protect data privacy and prevent unauthorized access to the system.

4. Reliability

- Ensure that the system operates consistently and can recover from failures without data loss or significant downtime.

5. Power Efficiency

- Optimize the power consumption of devices, especially for battery-powered sensors and actuators, to extend their operational lifespan.

Practical Example: Building a Simple IoT System

Let's build a simple IoT system that monitors temperature and humidity using an Arduino and an ESP8266 Wi-Fi module, and sends the data to a cloud platform for visualization.

Components Needed:

- Arduino Uno
- DHT11 temperature and humidity sensor
- ESP8266 Wi-Fi module
- Breadboard and jumper wires

Step-by-Step Instructions:

1. Set Up the Hardware

- Connect the DHT11 sensor to the Arduino:
  - VCC to 5V
  - GND to GND
  - Data pin to digital pin 2
- Connect the ESP8266 module to the Arduino:
  - VCC to 3.3V
  - GND to GND
  - TX to RX
  - RX to TX

2. Write the Arduino Code

```cpp
#include <DHT.h>
#include <ESP8266WiFi.h>
#include <WiFiClient.h>
#define DHTPIN 2 // DHT11 data pin
#define DHTTYPE DHT11
DHT dht(DHTPIN, DHTTYPE);
const char* ssid = "your_SSID";
const char* password = "your_PASSWORD";
const char* server = "api.example.com"; // Replace with your server
WiFiClient client;
void setup() {
Serial.begin(115200);
dht.begin();
WiFi.begin(ssid, password);
while (WiFi.status() != WL_CONNECTED) {
delay(500);
Serial.print(".");
}
Serial.println("WiFi connected");
}
void loop() {
float h = dht.readHumidity();
float t = dht.readTemperature();
if (isnan(h) || isnan(t)) {
Serial.println("Failed to read from DHT sensor!");
return;
}
if (client.connect(server, 80)) {
String postData = "temperature=" + String(t) + "&humidity=" +
String(h);
client.println("POST /data HTTP/1.1");
client.println("Host: api.example.com");
```

```
client.println("Content-Type: application/x-www-form-
urlencoded");
client.println("Connection: close");
client.println("Content-Length: " + String(postData.length()));
client.println();
client.print(postData);
client.stop();
}
delay(2000); // Send data every 2 seconds
}
```

3. Set Up the Cloud Platform

- Create an account on a cloud platform like ThingSpeak, AWS IoT, or similar.

- Create a new channel or device to receive data from your IoT system.

- Configure the server URL and API keys in the Arduino code.

4. Visualize the Data

- Use the cloud platform's dashboard to visualize the temperature and humidity data in real-time.

Summary

In this chapter, we explored the architecture of IoT systems, including the key components and design principles. Understanding the layered architecture of IoT systems helps in designing scalable, interoperable, secure, reliable, and power-efficient solutions. We also provided a practical example of building a simple IoT system to monitor temperature and humidity, demonstrating the integration of sensors, connectivity, data processing, and cloud services.

Keep Going!

You're making great progress in your journey to understand IoT systems! In the next chapter, we will delve into the hardware components used in IoT systems, including development boards, sensors, and actuators. Let's move on and start building more sophisticated IoT projects!

Chapter 3: Hardware for IoT
Introduction

In this chapter, we will explore the hardware components used in IoT systems. Understanding the various types of development boards, sensors, and actuators is crucial for designing and building effective IoT solutions. We will discuss the features and applications of popular IoT hardware, including Arduino, Raspberry Pi, ESP8266, ESP32, and a variety of sensors and actuators.

Development Boards

Development boards are the backbone of IoT projects, providing the processing power and connectivity needed to control sensors and actuators, process data, and communicate with other devices and systems. Here are some of the most commonly used development boards in IoT projects:

1. Arduino

- **Overview**: Arduino is an open-source electronics platform based on easy-to-use hardware and software. It is ideal for beginners and widely used in IoT projects.

- **Popular Models**: Arduino Uno, Arduino Nano, Arduino Mega.

- **Features**: Digital and analog I/O pins, USB interface for programming, support for various shields and modules.

- **Applications**: Prototyping, sensor data collection, home automation.

2. Raspberry Pi

- **Overview**: Raspberry Pi is a small, affordable computer that can be used for a wide range of IoT projects. It runs a full operating system (usually Linux) and supports various programming languages.

- **Popular Models**: Raspberry Pi 4, Raspberry Pi 3, Raspberry Pi Zero.

- **Features**: GPIO pins, HDMI output, USB ports, Ethernet, Wi-Fi, Bluetooth.

- **Applications**: Edge computing, media centers, home automation, robotics.

3. ESP8266

- **Overview**: ESP8266 is a low-cost Wi-Fi microchip with full TCP/IP stack and microcontroller capability. It is popular for IoT projects due to its affordability and ease of use.

- **Popular Models**: ESP-01, NodeMCU, Wemos D1 Mini.

- **Features**: Wi-Fi connectivity, GPIO pins, low power consumption, support for various development environments.

- **Applications**: Wireless sensor networks, smart home devices, data logging.

4. ESP32

- **Overview**: ESP32 is an upgrade to the ESP8266, offering dual-core processing, Bluetooth, and improved performance. It is versatile and powerful, suitable for more complex IoT projects.

- **Features**: Wi-Fi and Bluetooth connectivity, GPIO pins, dual-core processor, integrated sensors (touch, temperature, Hall effect).

- **Applications**: Wearable devices, industrial automation, wireless communication.

Sensors

Sensors are essential components in IoT systems, collecting data from the environment and converting it into electrical signals that can be processed by development boards. Here are some commonly used sensors in IoT projects:

1. Temperature Sensors

- **Types**: Thermistors, LM35, DS18B20.

- **Applications**: Environmental monitoring, HVAC systems, industrial processes.

2. Humidity Sensors

- **Types**: DHT11, DHT22, SHT31.
- **Applications**: Climate control, agriculture, weather stations.

3. Motion Sensors

- **Types**: Passive Infrared (PIR), ultrasonic, accelerometers.

- **Applications**: Security systems, human presence detection, activity monitoring.

4. Light Sensors

- **Types**: Photoresistors (LDR), photodiodes, TSL2561.

- **Applications**: Ambient light sensing, automatic lighting, solar energy systems.

5. Gas Sensors

- **Types**: MQ-series (MQ-2, MQ-7), CCS811.

- **Applications**: Air quality monitoring, gas leakage detection, industrial safety.

6. Proximity Sensors

- **Types**: Infrared (IR), ultrasonic, capacitive.

- **Applications**: Object detection, distance measurement, obstacle avoidance.

Actuators

Actuators are devices that convert electrical signals into physical actions, allowing IoT systems to interact with the environment. Here are some commonly used actuators in IoT projects:

1. Relays

- **Overview**: Relays are electrically operated switches that can control high-power devices with a low-power signal.

- **Applications**: Home automation, industrial control, remote switching.

2. Motors

- **Types**: DC motors, stepper motors, servo motors.
- **Applications**: Robotics, automation, precise positioning.

3. Solenoids

- **Overview**: Solenoids are electromechanical devices that convert electrical energy into linear motion.

- **Applications**: Door locks, valves, automotive systems.

4. LEDs

- **Overview**: LEDs (Light Emitting Diodes) are used for indication and illumination in IoT projects.

- **Applications**: Status indicators, lighting control, displays.

5. Buzzer

- **Overview**: Buzzers are used to generate sound alerts in IoT systems.
- **Applications**: Alarms, notifications, feedback systems.

Practical Example: Interfacing a Temperature Sensor with Arduino

Let's create a simple project to read temperature data from a DHT11 sensor and display it on the serial monitor using an Arduino.

Components Needed:

- Arduino Uno
- DHT11 temperature and humidity sensor
- Breadboard and jumper wires

Step-by-Step Instructions:
1. Set Up the Hardware

- Connect the DHT11 sensor to the Arduino:
  - VCC to 5V
  - GND to GND
  - Data pin to digital pin 2

2. Write the Arduino Code

```
#include <DHT.h>
#define DHTPIN 2 // DHT11 data pin
#define DHTTYPE DHT11
DHT dht(DHTPIN, DHTTYPE);
void setup() {
Serial.begin(9600);
dht.begin();
}
void loop() {
float h = dht.readHumidity();
float t = dht.readTemperature();
if (isnan(h) || isnan(t)) {
Serial.println("Failed to read from DHT sensor!");
return;
}
Serial.print("Humidity: ");
Serial.print(h);
Serial.print(" %\t");
Serial.print("Temperature: ");
Serial.print(t);
Serial.println(" *C");
delay(2000); // Wait a few seconds between readings
}
```

3. Upload the Code and Test

- Open the Arduino IDE, upload the code to the Arduino board, and open the Serial Monitor to see the temperature and humidity readings.

Summary

In this chapter, we explored the hardware components used in IoT systems, including development boards, sensors, and actuators. Understanding the features and applications of these components is crucial for designing and building effective IoT solutions. We also provided a practical example of interfacing a temperature sensor with an Arduino, demonstrating how to collect and display sensor data.

Keep Going!

You're making great progress in your journey to understand IoT systems! In the next chapter, we will delve into communication protocols, exploring how IoT devices communicate with each other and with cloud platforms. Let's move on and start connecting your IoT devices to the world!

Chapter 4: Communication Protocols Introduction

Communication protocols are the backbone of IoT systems, enabling devices to exchange data and commands. In this chapter, we will explore various communication protocols used in IoT, including MQTT, CoAP, HTTP, and WebSockets. We will also discuss different connectivity options such as Wi-Fi, Bluetooth, Zigbee, LoRa, and cellular networks. Understanding these protocols and connectivity options will help you design robust and efficient IoT systems.

Overview of IoT Communication Protocols

1. MQTT (Message Queuing Telemetry Transport)

- **Overview**: MQTT is a lightweight, publish-subscribe network protocol that transports messages between devices. It is designed for connections with remote locations where a small code footprint is required or network bandwidth is limited.

- **Use Cases**: Home automation, telemetry, sensor networks.

- **Key Features**: Low bandwidth usage, QoS levels, retained messages.

2. CoAP (Constrained Application Protocol)

- **Overview**: CoAP is a specialized web transfer protocol for use with constrained nodes and networks in the Internet of Things. It is designed to enable simple, constrained devices to join the IoT.

● **Use Cases**: Resource-constrained environments, low-power devices.

● **Key Features**: RESTful architecture, multicast support, low overhead.

3. HTTP (Hypertext Transfer Protocol)

● **Overview**: HTTP is a widely used protocol for transmitting hypermedia documents, such as HTML. It is the foundation of any data exchange on the Web and can be used for IoT applications.

● **Use Cases**: Web-based IoT applications, RESTful APIs.

● **Key Features**: Stateless, simple, widely supported.

4. WebSockets

● **Overview**: WebSockets provide full-duplex communication channels over a single TCP connection. They are designed to be implemented in web browsers and web servers but can be used by any client or server application.

● **Use Cases**: Real-time applications, live data streaming.

● **Key Features**: Low latency, full-duplex communication, persistent connection.

Connectivity Options

1. Wi-Fi

- **Overview**: Wi-Fi is a wireless networking technology that allows devices to communicate without direct cable connections. It is widely used in IoT for its high data rate and wide availability.

- **Use Cases**: Home automation, smart appliances, video surveillance.

- **Key Features**: High data rate, wide coverage, easy integration.

2. Bluetooth

- **Overview**: Bluetooth is a wireless technology standard for exchanging data over short distances. It is commonly used for personal area networks and connecting devices within a short range.

- **Use Cases**: Wearable devices, health monitoring, personal gadgets.

- **Key Features**: Low power consumption, short-range communication, peer-to-peer connectivity.

3. Zigbee

- **Overview**: Zigbee is a specification for a suite of high-level communication protocols using low-power digital radios. It is intended for low-data rate, low-power applications.

- **Use Cases**: Smart lighting, home automation, industrial control.

- **Key Features**: Low power, mesh networking, secure.

4. LoRa (Long Range)

- **Overview**: LoRa is a long-range, low-power wireless platform that targets applications for the Internet of Things. It is ideal for use in wide-area networks and long-distance communication.

- **Use Cases**: Smart cities, agriculture, asset tracking.

- **Key Features**: Long range, low power, wide-area coverage.

5. Cellular Networks

- **Overview**: Cellular networks provide wireless communication over large geographic areas. They are suitable for IoT applications that require mobility and wide coverage.

- **Use Cases**: Connected vehicles, remote monitoring, asset tracking.

- **Key Features**: Wide coverage, high data rate, support for mobility.

Implementing Communication Protocols with Arduino

Let's implement a simple project to send sensor data from an Arduino to a cloud server using the MQTT protocol. We will use an ESP8266 Wi-Fi module for connectivity.

Components Needed:

- Arduino Uno
- ESP8266 Wi-Fi module
- DHT11 temperature and humidity sensor
- Breadboard and jumper wires

Step-by-Step Instructions:

1. Set Up the Hardware

- Connect the DHT11 sensor to the Arduino:
  - VCC to 5V
  - GND to GND
  - Data pin to digital pin 2
- Connect the ESP8266 module to the Arduino:
  - VCC to 3.3V
  - GND to GND
  - TX to RX (through a voltage divider)
  - RX to TX

2. Write the Arduino Code

```cpp
#include <ESP8266WiFi.h>
#include <PubSubClient.h>
#include <DHT.h>
#define DHTPIN 2 // DHT11 data pin
#define DHTTYPE DHT11
DHT dht(DHTPIN, DHTTYPE);
const char* ssid = "your_SSID";
const char* password = "your_PASSWORD";
const char* mqttServer = "broker.hivemq.com";
const int mqttPort = 1883;
const char* mqttUser = "your_MQTT_username"; // Optional
const char* mqttPassword = "your_MQTT_password"; // Optional
WiFiClient espClient;
PubSubClient client(espClient);
void setup() {
Serial.begin(115200);
dht.begin();
WiFi.begin(ssid, password);
while (WiFi.status() != WL_CONNECTED) {
delay(500);
Serial.print(".");
}
Serial.println("WiFi connected");
client.setServer(mqttServer, mqttPort);
while (!client.connected()) {
Serial.println("Connecting to MQTT...");
if (client.connect("ESP8266Client", mqttUser, mqttPassword)) {
Serial.println("Connected to MQTT");
} else {
Serial.print("Failed with state ");
Serial.print(client.state());
delay(2000);
```

```
}
}
}
void loop() {
float h = dht.readHumidity();
float t = dht.readTemperature();
if (isnan(h) || isnan(t)) {
Serial.println("Failed to read from DHT sensor!");
return;
}
String payload = "temperature:" + String(t) + ",humidity:" +
String(h);
client.publish("iot/sensors", payload.c_str());
delay(2000); // Wait a few seconds between readings
}
```

3. Upload the Code and Test

- Open the Arduino IDE, upload the code to the Arduino board, and monitor the serial output to see the connection status and published messages.

4. Monitor the MQTT Broker

- Use an MQTT client (such as MQTT.fx or a web-based client) to subscribe to the "iot/sensors" topic and monitor the published sensor data.

Summary

In this chapter, we explored various communication protocols and connectivity options used in IoT systems. Understanding these protocols is crucial for designing robust and efficient IoT solutions. We also provided a practical example of sending sensor data from an Arduino to a cloud server using MQTT, demonstrating how to implement communication protocols in your IoT projects.

Keep Going!

You're making great progress in your journey to understand IoT systems! In the next chapter, we will delve into data acquisition and processing, exploring how to collect, process, and store data from your IoT devices. Let's move on and start working with IoT data!

Chapter 5: Data Acquisition and Processing

Introduction

Data acquisition and processing are fundamental aspects of IoT systems. In this chapter, we will explore techniques for collecting, processing, and storing data from IoT devices. We will discuss local data processing on edge devices, sending data to the cloud, and utilizing cloud-based storage and analytics services. Understanding these processes is crucial for making intelligent decisions based on the data collected by your IoT system.

Data Collection Techniques

1. Sampling and Sensing

- **Overview**: Sampling involves measuring physical quantities at regular intervals using sensors. Proper sampling rates ensure accurate data representation.

- **Techniques**:

  ○ **Analog Sensors**: Convert physical quantities to analog signals (e.g., temperature sensors, light sensors).

  ○ **Digital Sensors**: Provide data in digital form (e.g., digital temperature sensors, digital accelerometers).

2. Local Data Processing

● **Overview**: Processing data locally on edge devices reduces latency and bandwidth usage by performing initial filtering, aggregation, and analysis.

● **Techniques**:

○ **Filtering**: Removing noise and irrelevant data.

○ **Aggregation**: Summarizing data over time or across multiple sensors.

○ **Thresholding**: Triggering actions based on predefined thresholds.

Sending Data to the Cloud

1. Connectivity Options

● **Overview**: Choose appropriate connectivity options (e.g., Wi-Fi, Bluetooth, LoRa, cellular) based on range, power consumption, and data rate requirements.

● **Techniques**:

○ **Wi-Fi**: High data rate, suitable for home and office environments.

○ **Bluetooth**: Short-range, low power, ideal for personal devices.

○ **LoRa**: Long-range, low power, suitable for wide-area networks.

○ **Cellular**: Wide coverage, suitable for mobile and remote applications.

2. Data Transmission Protocols

● **Overview**: Use protocols like MQTT, HTTP, and CoAP to transmit data from edge devices to cloud servers.

● **Techniques**:

○ **MQTT**: Lightweight, publish-subscribe protocol suitable for low-bandwidth networks.

○ **HTTP**: Widely used, stateless protocol suitable for web-based applications.

○ **CoAP**: Lightweight protocol designed for constrained devices and networks.

3. Secure Data Transmission

● **Overview**: Ensure data integrity and privacy by encrypting data during transmission.

● **Techniques**:

○ **TLS/SSL**: Use Transport Layer Security (TLS) or Secure Sockets Layer (SSL) to encrypt data.

○ **Authentication**: Implement authentication mechanisms to verify device identity.

Cloud Platforms for IoT

1. Overview of Popular IoT Cloud Platforms

• **AWS IoT**: Amazon Web Services platform for IoT, offering device management, data processing, and analytics.

• **Azure IoT**: Microsoft's IoT suite providing device connectivity, data storage, and advanced analytics.

• **Google Cloud IoT**: Google's platform for managing IoT devices and processing IoT data.

2. Setting Up IoT Devices on Cloud Platforms

• **AWS IoT**: Register your device, configure security certificates, and set up MQTT topics.

• **Azure IoT**: Create an IoT Hub, register your device, and configure message routing.

• **Google Cloud IoT**: Create a registry, register your device, and set up Pub/Sub topics.

3. Data Storage and Analytics

• **Overview**: Utilize cloud-based storage solutions to store IoT data and leverage analytics services to gain insights.

• **Techniques**:

○ **Time-Series Databases**: Store time-stamped data efficiently (e.g., Amazon Timestream, InfluxDB).

○ **Big Data Analytics**: Analyze large volumes of data using tools like AWS Redshift, Azure Synapse, or Google BigQuery.

○ **Machine Learning**: Apply machine learning models to IoT data for predictive analytics and anomaly detection.

Practical Example: Sending Data to AWS IoT

Let's create a simple project to send temperature and humidity data from an Arduino to AWS IoT.

Components Needed:

- Arduino Uno
- ESP8266 Wi-Fi module
- DHT11 temperature and humidity sensor
- Breadboard and jumper wires

Step-by-Step Instructions:
1. Set Up the Hardware

- Connect the DHT11 sensor to the Arduino:
○ VCC to 5V
○ GND to GND
○ Data pin to digital pin 2
- Connect the ESP8266 module to the Arduino:
○ VCC to 3.3V
○ GND to GND
○ TX to RX (through a voltage divider)
○ RX to TX

2. Set Up AWS IoT

- **Create an AWS Account**: If you don't have one, sign up atAWS[1].

- **Set Up AWS IoT Core**:

---

1. https://aws.amazon.com/

○ Go to the AWS IoT Core console.

○ Create a new thing (device) and download the security certificates.

○ Attach a policy to your thing that allows it to publish and subscribe to MQTT topics.

● **Configure MQTT Client:**

○ Use the AWS IoT endpoint and device certificates in your Arduino code.

3. Write the Arduino Code

```cpp
#include <ESP8266WiFi.h>
#include <PubSubClient.h>
#include <DHT.h>
#define DHTPIN 2 // DHT11 data pin
#define DHTTYPE DHT11
DHT dht(DHTPIN, DHTTYPE);
const char* ssid = "your_SSID";
const char* password = "your_PASSWORD";
const char* mqttServer = "your-aws-iot-endpoint";
const int mqttPort = 8883;
const char* mqttClientID = "your-client-id";
const char* mqttTopic = "iot/sensors";
// Your AWS IoT certificates
const char* ca_cert = \
"——-BEGIN CERTIFICATE——-\n" \
"YOUR_CA_CERT_HERE\n" \
"——-END CERTIFICATE——-";
const char* client_cert = \
"——-BEGIN CERTIFICATE——-\n" \
"YOUR_CLIENT_CERT_HERE\n" \
"——-END CERTIFICATE——-";
const char* private_key = \
"——-BEGIN PRIVATE KEY——-\n" \
"YOUR_PRIVATE_KEY_HERE\n" \
"——-END PRIVATE KEY——-";
WiFiClientSecure espClient;
PubSubClient client(espClient);
void setup() {
Serial.begin(115200);
dht.begin();
WiFi.begin(ssid, password);
while (WiFi.status() != WL_CONNECTED) {
```

```cpp
delay(500);
Serial.print(".");
}
Serial.println("WiFi connected");
espClient.setCACert(ca_cert);
espClient.setCertificate(client_cert);
espClient.setPrivateKey(private_key);
client.setServer(mqttServer, mqttPort);
while (!client.connected()) {
Serial.println("Connecting to MQTT...");
if (client.connect(mqttClientID)) {
Serial.println("Connected to MQTT");
} else {
Serial.print("Failed with state ");
Serial.print(client.state());
delay(2000);
}
}
}
void loop() {
float h = dht.readHumidity();
float t = dht.readTemperature();
if (isnan(h) || isnan(t)) {
Serial.println("Failed to read from DHT sensor!");
return;
}
String payload = "{\"temperature\":" + String(t) + ",\"humidity\":" +
String(h) + "}";
client.publish(mqttTopic, payload.c_str());
delay(2000); // Wait a few seconds between readings
}
```

4. Upload the Code and Test

- Open the Arduino IDE, upload the code to the Arduino board, and monitor the serial output to see the connection status and published messages.

5. Monitor Data on AWS IoT

- Go to the AWS IoT Core console and navigate to the MQTT test client.

- Subscribe to the "iot/sensors" topic to see the incoming data from your Arduino.

Summary

In this chapter, we explored data acquisition and processing techniques in IoT systems. We discussed local data processing, sending data to the cloud, and utilizing cloud platforms for storage and analytics. We also provided a practical example of sending sensor data from an Arduino to AWS IoT, demonstrating how to implement data acquisition and processing in your IoT projects.

Keep Going!

You're making great progress in your journey to understand IoT systems! In the next chapter, we will delve into cloud platforms for IoT, exploring how to leverage cloud services for managing, storing, and analyzing IoT data. Let's move on and start connecting your IoT devices to the cloud!

Chapter 6: Cloud Platforms for IoT Introduction

Cloud platforms are integral to IoT systems, providing the infrastructure for data storage, processing, and analytics. In this chapter, we will explore some of the most popular IoT cloud platforms, including AWS IoT, Azure IoT, and Google Cloud IoT. We will discuss how to set up IoT devices on these platforms, manage data storage, and utilize analytics services to gain insights from IoT data.

Overview of Popular IoT Cloud Platforms

1. AWS IoT (Amazon Web Services Internet of Things)

- **Overview**: AWS IoT provides secure, bi-directional communication between IoT devices and the AWS cloud. It supports device management, data processing, and advanced analytics.

- **Key Features:**

  o Device Management: Register, organize, and manage IoT devices at scale.

  o Secure Communication: Ensure data privacy and integrity with TLS encryption.

  o Data Processing: Process and act upon device data using AWS Lambda.

  o Analytics: Gain insights from IoT data with AWS IoT Analytics and Amazon QuickSight.

2. Azure IoT (Microsoft Azure Internet of Things)

- **Overview**: Azure IoT Suite provides a comprehensive set of services for connecting, monitoring, and managing IoT assets. It includes device provisioning, data storage, and advanced analytics.

- **Key Features**:

  - IoT Hub: Centralized service for bi-directional communication between IoT applications and devices.

  - Device Provisioning Service: Securely provision and register IoT devices at scale.

  - Stream Analytics: Real-time data stream processing and analytics.

  - Time Series Insights: Interactive analytics and visualization of time-series data.

3. Google Cloud IoT

- **Overview**: Google Cloud IoT offers a set of fully managed services for connecting, managing, and ingesting data from IoT devices. It integrates with other Google Cloud services for data processing and machine learning.

- **Key Features**:

  - IoT Core: Secure device connection and management.

  - Pub/Sub: Reliable, scalable messaging for event-driven systems.

○ Dataflow: Real-time data processing and analytics.

○ BigQuery: Scalable data warehouse for querying and analyzing large datasets.

Setting Up IoT Devices on Cloud Platforms

1. AWS IoT
Step-by-Step Instructions:
a. Create an AWS Account

● Sign up for an AWS account atAWS[1].

b. Set Up AWS IoT Core

● Go to the AWS IoT Core console.

● Create a new thing (device).

● Download the security certificates (public key, private key, and root CA certificate).

● Attach a policy to your thing that allows it to publish and subscribe to MQTT topics.

c. Configure MQTT Client in Arduino

● Use the downloaded certificates and AWS IoT endpoint in your Arduino code.

Example Code:

```cpp
#include <ESP8266WiFi.h>
#include <PubSubClient.h>
#include <DHT.h>
#define DHTPIN 2
#define DHTTYPE DHT11
DHT dht(DHTPIN, DHTTYPE);
const char* ssid = "your_SSID";
const char* password = "your_PASSWORD";
const char* mqttServer = "your-aws-iot-endpoint";
const int mqttPort = 8883;
const char* mqttClientID = "your-client-id";
const char* mqttTopic = "iot/sensors";
const char* ca_cert = \
"——-BEGIN CERTIFICATE——-\n" \
"YOUR_CA_CERT_HERE\n" \
"——-END CERTIFICATE——-";
const char* client_cert = \
"——-BEGIN CERTIFICATE——-\n" \
"YOUR_CLIENT_CERT_HERE\n" \
"——-END CERTIFICATE——-";
const char* private_key = \
"——-BEGIN PRIVATE KEY——-\n" \
"YOUR_PRIVATE_KEY_HERE\n" \
"——-END PRIVATE KEY——-";
WiFiClientSecure espClient;
PubSubClient client(espClient);
void setup() {
Serial.begin(115200);
dht.begin();
WiFi.begin(ssid, password);
while (WiFi.status() != WL_CONNECTED) {
delay(500);
```

```cpp
Serial.print(".");
}
Serial.println("WiFi connected");
espClient.setCACert(ca_cert);
espClient.setCertificate(client_cert);
espClient.setPrivateKey(private_key);
client.setServer(mqttServer, mqttPort);
while (!client.connected()) {
Serial.println("Connecting to MQTT...");
if (client.connect(mqttClientID)) {
Serial.println("Connected to MQTT");
} else {
Serial.print("Failed with state ");
Serial.print(client.state());
delay(2000);
}
}
}
void loop() {
float h = dht.readHumidity();
float t = dht.readTemperature();
if (isnan(h) || isnan(t)) {
Serial.println("Failed to read from DHT sensor!");
return;
}
String payload = "{\"temperature\":" + String(t) + ",\"humidity\":" +
String(h) + "}";
client.publish(mqttTopic, payload.c_str());
delay(2000);
}
```

d. Monitor Data on AWS IoT

- Use the MQTT test client in the AWS IoT Core console to subscribe to the "iot/sensors" topic and see the data.

2. Azure IoT
Step-by-Step Instructions:
a. Create an Azure Account

- Sign up for an Azure account atAzure[2].

b. Set Up Azure IoT Hub

- Go to the Azure portal and create a new IoT Hub.
- Register your device in the IoT Hub.
- Download the connection string for your device.

c. Configure MQTT Client in Arduino

- Use the downloaded connection string in your Arduino code.

Example Code:

---

2. https://azure.microsoft.com/

```cpp
#include <WiFi.h>
#include <AzureIoTHub.h>
#include <DHT.h>
#define DHTPIN 2
#define DHTTYPE DHT11
DHT dht(DHTPIN, DHTTYPE);
const char* ssid = "your_SSID";
const char* password = "your_PASSWORD";
const char* connectionString = "HostName=your-iot-hub.azure-
devices.net;DeviceId=your-device-id;SharedAccessKey=your-access-
key";
void setup() {
Serial.begin(115200);
dht.begin();
WiFi.begin(ssid, password);
while (WiFi.status() != WL_CONNECTED) {
delay(500);
Serial.print(".");
}
Serial.println("WiFi connected");
if (IoTHub_Init() != 0) {
Serial.println("Failed to initialize IoT Hub");
}
}
void loop() {
float h = dht.readHumidity();
float t = dht.readTemperature();
if (isnan(h) || isnan(t)) {
Serial.println("Failed to read from DHT sensor!");
return;
}
IOTHUB_MESSAGE_HANDLE messageHandle;
```

```
char messagePayload[128];
snprintf(messagePayload, sizeof(messagePayload),
"{\"temperature\":%f,\"humidity\":%f}", t, h);
messageHandle =
IoTHubMessage_CreateFromString(messagePayload);
if (IoTHubDeviceClient_SendEventAsync(deviceHandle,
messageHandle, NULL, NULL) != IOTHUB_CLIENT_OK) {
Serial.println("Failed to send message");
} else {
Serial.println("Message sent");
}
IoTHubMessage_Destroy(messageHandle);
delay(2000);
}
```

d. Monitor Data on Azure IoT

- Use the Azure IoT Explorer tool to monitor messages sent to the IoT Hub.

3. Google Cloud IoT
Step-by-Step Instructions:
a. Create a Google Cloud Account

- Sign up for a Google Cloud account atGoogle Cloud[3].

b. Set Up Google Cloud IoT Core

- Go to the Google Cloud Console and create a new project.
- Enable the Cloud IoT Core API.
- Create a registry and register your device.
- Generate and download the device keys.

---

3. https://cloud.google.com/

c. Configure MQTT Client in Arduino

- Use the device keys and Google Cloud IoT endpoint in your Arduino code.

Example Code:

```cpp
#include <WiFi.h>
#include <CloudIoTCore.h>
#include <CloudIoTCoreMqtt.h>
#include <DHT.h>
#define DHTPIN 2
#define DHTTYPE DHT11
DHT dht(DHTPIN, DHTTYPE);
const char* ssid = "your_SSID";
const char* password = "your_PASSWORD";
const char* project_id = "your-project-id";
const char* location = "your-region";
const char* registry_id = "your-registry-id";
const char* device_id = "your-device-id";
// Path to private key file
const char* private_key_str = "your-private-key";
// Time (seconds) to expire token += 20 minutes
const int jwt_exp_secs = 3600; // Maximum 24H (3600*24)
WiFiClientSecure netClient;
CloudIoTCoreDevice device(project_id, location, registry_id,
device_id, private_key_str);
CloudIoTCoreMqtt mqttClient(&netClient, &device);
void setup() {
Serial.begin(115200);
dht.begin();
WiFi.begin(ssid, password);
while (WiFi.status() != WL_CONNECTED) {
delay(500);
Serial.print(".");
}
Serial.println("WiFi connected");
device.setJwtExpSecs(jwt_exp_secs);
mqttClient.startMQTT();
```

```
}
void loop() {
mqttClient.loop();
float h = dht.readHumidity();
float t = dht.readTemperature();
if (isnan(h) || isnan(t)) {
Serial.println("Failed to read from DHT sensor!");
return;
}
String payload = "{\"temperature\":" + String(t) + ",\"humidity\":" +
String(h) + "}";
mqttClient.publishTelemetry(payload);
delay(2000);
}
```

d. Monitor Data on Google Cloud IoT

- Use the Google Cloud Console to subscribe to the Pub/
Sub topic and monitor the incoming messages.

Summary

In this chapter, we explored how to set up IoT devices on popular cloud platforms such as AWS IoT, Azure IoT, and Google Cloud IoT. We discussed the key features of these platforms and provided step-by-step instructions for connecting IoT devices and sending data to the cloud. By leveraging cloud services, you can manage, store, and analyze IoT data efficiently, enabling advanced applications and insights.

Keep Going!

You're making great progress in your journey to understand IoT systems! In the next chapter, we will delve into security in IoT, exploring best practices and techniques to protect your IoT devices and data. Let's move on and ensure your IoT systems are secure!

Chapter 7: Security in IoT
Introduction

Security is a critical aspect of IoT systems, as they often involve sensitive data and control over physical devices. Ensuring the security of your IoT devices and data is essential to protect against unauthorized access, data breaches, and other threats. In this chapter, we will explore the challenges of IoT security, best practices, and techniques to secure your IoT systems.

Understanding IoT Security Challenges

1. Limited Resources

- IoT devices often have limited processing power, memory, and storage, making it challenging to implement robust security measures.

2. Large Attack Surface

- The vast number of interconnected devices increases the potential points of attack, making it difficult to secure every entry point.

3. Diverse Ecosystem

- The variety of devices, operating systems, and communication protocols in IoT systems complicates the implementation of consistent security practices.

4. Physical Exposure

- Many IoT devices are deployed in easily accessible locations, increasing the risk of physical tampering.

Best Practices for Securing IoT Devices

1. Secure Boot

- Ensure that devices boot using only trusted software by implementing secure boot mechanisms that verify the integrity of the firmware.

2. Device Authentication

- Use strong authentication mechanisms to verify the identity of devices before allowing them to connect to the network.

3. Data Encryption

- Encrypt data both at rest and in transit to protect it from unauthorized access and tampering.

4. Regular Firmware Updates

- Keep device firmware up-to-date with the latest security patches and features to protect against known vulnerabilities.

5. Network Security

- Implement network security measures such as firewalls, intrusion detection systems, and secure communication protocols to protect against network-based attacks.

6. Secure Communication Protocols

- Use secure communication protocols such as TLS/SSL for data transmission to ensure data integrity and confidentiality.

7. Access Control

- Implement strict access control policies to limit access to IoT devices and data to authorized users and applications.

Implementing Security in IoT Projects

1. Secure Boot with Arduino

- Use a hardware-based secure boot mechanism to ensure that only trusted firmware is loaded on the device.

- Example: Use an external secure element (e.g., ATECC608A) to verify the firmware signature during boot.

2. Device Authentication with ESP8266

- Implement mutual authentication between the device and the server using X.509 certificates.

- Example: Use the ESP8266's secure Wi-Fi features to connect to a server using TLS with client certificates.

3. Data Encryption with AES

- Encrypt sensitive data stored on the device or transmitted over the network using AES (Advanced Encryption Standard).

● Example: Use the Arduino Crypto library to implement AES encryption for sensor data.

4. Secure Communication with MQTT over TLS

● Use the MQTT protocol with TLS encryption to securely transmit data between IoT devices and the cloud.

● Example: Configure the PubSubClient library in Arduino to use TLS for secure MQTT communication.

Code Example: Secure MQTT Communication with TLS

```cpp
#include <ESP8266WiFi.h>
#include <PubSubClient.h>
#include <DHT.h>
#define DHTPIN 2
#define DHTTYPE DHT11
DHT dht(DHTPIN, DHTTYPE);
const char* ssid = "your_SSID";
const char* password = "your_PASSWORD";
const char* mqttServer = "your-aws-iot-endpoint";
const int mqttPort = 8883;
const char* mqttClientID = "your-client-id";
const char* mqttTopic = "iot/sensors";
const char* ca_cert = \
"——-BEGIN CERTIFICATE——-\n" \
"YOUR_CA_CERT_HERE\n" \
"——-END CERTIFICATE——-";
const char* client_cert = \
"——-BEGIN CERTIFICATE——-\n" \
"YOUR_CLIENT_CERT_HERE\n" \
"——-END CERTIFICATE——-";
const char* private_key = \
"——-BEGIN PRIVATE KEY——-\n" \
"YOUR_PRIVATE_KEY_HERE\n" \
"——-END PRIVATE KEY——-";
WiFiClientSecure espClient;
PubSubClient client(espClient);
void setup() {
Serial.begin(115200);
dht.begin();
WiFi.begin(ssid, password);
while (WiFi.status() != WL_CONNECTED) {
delay(500);
```

```
Serial.print(".");
}
Serial.println("WiFi connected");
espClient.setCACert(ca_cert);
espClient.setCertificate(client_cert);
espClient.setPrivateKey(private_key);
client.setServer(mqttServer, mqttPort);
while (!client.connected()) {
Serial.println("Connecting to MQTT...");
if (client.connect(mqttClientID)) {
Serial.println("Connected to MQTT");
} else {
Serial.print("Failed with state ");
Serial.print(client.state());
delay(2000);
}
}
}
void loop() {
float h = dht.readHumidity();
float t = dht.readTemperature();
if (isnan(h) || isnan(t)) {
Serial.println("Failed to read from DHT sensor!");
return;
}
String payload = "{\"temperature\":" + String(t) + ",\"humidity\":" +
String(h) + "}";
client.publish(mqttTopic, payload.c_str());
delay(2000);
}
```

5. Regular Firmware Updates with OTA (Over-the-Air)

• Implement OTA updates to regularly update device firmware without physical access.

• Example: Use the ArduinoOTA library to enable OTA firmware updates for ESP8266 and ESP32 devices.

6. Network Security with Firewalls

• Configure network firewalls to monitor and control incoming and outgoing network traffic based on predetermined security rules.

• Example: Use a router with built-in firewall capabilities to secure the IoT network.

Example: Secure Data Transmission with TLS on ESP32

```cpp
#include <WiFi.h>
#include <PubSubClient.h>
#include <DHT.h>
#define DHTPIN 2
#define DHTTYPE DHT11
DHT dht(DHTPIN, DHTTYPE);
const char* ssid = "your_SSID";
const char* password = "your_PASSWORD";
const char* mqttServer = "your-aws-iot-endpoint";
const int mqttPort = 8883;
const char* mqttClientID = "your-client-id";
const char* mqttTopic = "iot/sensors";
const char* ca_cert = \
"——-BEGIN CERTIFICATE——-\n" \
"YOUR_CA_CERT_HERE\n" \
"——-END CERTIFICATE——-";
const char* client_cert = \
"——-BEGIN CERTIFICATE——-\n" \
"YOUR_CLIENT_CERT_HERE\n" \
"——-END CERTIFICATE——-";
const char* private_key = \
"——-BEGIN PRIVATE KEY——-\n" \
"YOUR_PRIVATE_KEY_HERE\n" \
"——-END PRIVATE KEY——-";
WiFiClientSecure espClient;
PubSubClient client(espClient);
void setup() {
Serial.begin(115200);
dht.begin();
WiFi.begin(ssid, password);
while (WiFi.status() != WL_CONNECTED) {
delay(500);
```

```cpp
Serial.print(".");
}
Serial.println("WiFi connected");
espClient.setCACert(ca_cert);
espClient.setCertificate(client_cert);
espClient.setPrivateKey(private_key);
client.setServer(mqttServer, mqttPort);
while (!client.connected()) {
Serial.println("Connecting to MQTT...");
if (client.connect(mqttClientID)) {
Serial.println("Connected to MQTT");
} else {
Serial.print("Failed with state ");
Serial.print(client.state());
delay(2000);
}
}
}
void loop() {
float h = dht.readHumidity();
float t = dht.readTemperature();
if (isnan(h) || isnan(t)) {
Serial.println("Failed to read from DHT sensor!");
return;
}
String payload = "{\"temperature\":" + String(t) + ",\"humidity\":" +
String(h) + "}";
client.publish(mqttTopic, payload.c_str());
delay(2000);
}
```

Summary

In this chapter, we explored the importance of security in IoT systems and the challenges associated with it. We discussed best practices for securing IoT devices, including secure boot, device authentication, data encryption, regular firmware updates, network security, and secure communication protocols. Implementing these practices will help protect your IoT systems from unauthorized access and data breaches.

Keep Going!

You're making great progress in your journey to understand IoT systems! In the next chapter, we will delve into advanced IoT concepts, including edge computing, machine learning, and IoT interoperability. Let's move on and explore these exciting topics!

Chapter 8: Advanced IoT Concepts

Introduction

In this chapter, we will explore advanced IoT concepts that are shaping the future of interconnected systems. We will discuss edge computing, machine learning in IoT, and IoT interoperability. These advanced topics will help you understand the evolving landscape of IoT and how to leverage these technologies for more sophisticated applications.

Edge Computing

1. Overview

- **Definition**: Edge computing refers to the processing of data near the source of data generation (i.e., at the edge of the network) rather than in a centralized cloud. This approach reduces latency, bandwidth usage, and enhances real-time data processing.

- **Benefits:**

  ○ **Reduced Latency**: Faster response times by processing data closer to the source.

  ○ **Bandwidth Optimization**: Reduces the amount of data transmitted to the cloud.

  ○ **Enhanced Privacy**: Keeps sensitive data local, reducing exposure to potential breaches.

2. Use Cases

- **Industrial IoT**: Real-time monitoring and control of industrial equipment.

- **Smart Cities**: Traffic management systems that process data locally for real-time adjustments.

- **Healthcare**: Wearable devices that analyze patient data in real-time for immediate feedback.

3. Practical Example: Edge Computing with Raspberry Pi Let's implement a simple edge computing solution to process and analyze temperature data locally using a Raspberry Pi.

Components Needed:

- Raspberry Pi
- DHT22 temperature and humidity sensor
- Jumper wires

Step-by-Step Instructions:
a. Set Up the Hardware

- Connect the DHT22 sensor to the Raspberry Pi:
- VCC to 3.3V
- GND to GND
- Data pin to GPIO4

b. Install Required Libraries

- Install the Adafruit DHT library for Python.

sh

sudo pip3 install Adafruit_DHT

c. Write the Python Code

```python
import Adafruit_DHT
import time
DHT_SENSOR = Adafruit_DHT.DHT22
DHT_PIN = 4
while True:
    humidity, temperature = Adafruit_DHT.read(DHT_SENSOR, DHT_PIN)
    if humidity is not None and temperature is not None:
        print(f"Temp={temperature:.1f}C Humidity={humidity:.1f}%")
    else:
        print("Failed to retrieve data from humidity sensor")
    time.sleep(2)
```

d. Run the Code

- Execute the Python script to see real-time temperature and humidity data processed locally on the Raspberry Pi.

```sh
python3 dht22_example.py
```

Machine Learning in IoT

1. Overview

- **Definition**: Machine learning (ML) in IoT involves using algorithms to analyze and learn from IoT data, enabling predictive maintenance, anomaly detection, and intelligent decision-making.

- **Benefits:**

  ○ **Predictive Maintenance**: Forecast equipment failures before they occur.

○ **Anomaly Detection**: Identify unusual patterns or behaviors in data.

○ **Automation**: Automate decision-making processes based on data insights.

2. Use Cases

• **Smart Homes**: Personalize home automation based on user behavior.

• **Agriculture**: Optimize crop yield by analyzing environmental data.

• **Healthcare**: Predict health issues based on patient data from wearable devices.

3. Practical Example: Anomaly Detection in Sensor Data Let's implement a simple anomaly detection system using Python and a temperature sensor.

Components Needed:

• Arduino Uno
• DHT11 temperature and humidity sensor
• Breadboard and jumper wires
• Python environment with scikit-learn library

Step-by-Step Instructions:
a. Collect Data with Arduino

• Use the Arduino to collect temperature data and send it to a computer via serial communication.

```
#include <DHT.h>
#define DHTPIN 2
#define DHTTYPE DHT11
DHT dht(DHTPIN, DHTTYPE);
void setup() {
Serial.begin(9600);
dht.begin();
}
void loop() {
float temperature = dht.readTemperature();
if (!isnan(temperature)) {
Serial.println(temperature);
}
delay(2000);
}
```

b. Read Data in Python

- Use Python to read temperature data from the Arduino and detect anomalies using the Isolation Forest algorithm.

```python
import serial
import time
import numpy as np
from sklearn.ensemble import IsolationForest
ser = serial.Serial('COM3', 9600) # Adjust COM port as needed
# Collect data
data = []
start_time = time.time()
while time.time() - start_time < 60: # Collect data for 60 seconds
line = ser.readline().decode('utf-8').strip()
try:
temperature = float(line)
data.append([temperature])
except ValueError:
continue
# Convert to numpy array
data = np.array(data)
# Train Isolation Forest model
model = IsolationForest(contamination=0.1)
model.fit(data)
# Predict anomalies
predictions = model.predict(data)
anomalies = data[predictions == -1]
# Print anomalies
print("Anomalies detected:")
for anomaly in anomalies:
print(anomaly)
ser.close()
```

IoT Interoperability

1. Overview

- **Definition**: IoT interoperability refers to the ability of different IoT systems and devices to communicate and work together seamlessly.

- **Benefits**:

  ○ **Flexibility**: Integrate devices from different manufacturers.

  ○ **Scalability**: Easily expand and upgrade IoT systems.

  ○ **Efficiency**: Simplify management and data exchange between devices.

2. Standards and Protocols

- **MQTT**: Lightweight messaging protocol for small sensors and mobile devices.

- **CoAP**: Specialized web transfer protocol for use with constrained nodes.

- **Zigbee**: Wireless mesh protocol for low-power devices.

- **OPC UA**: Standard for secure and reliable data exchange in industrial automation.

3. Practical Example: Integrating MQTT and CoAP Devices

Let's create a bridge between an MQTT and a CoAP device using a Raspberry Pi as the intermediary.

Components Needed:

- Raspberry Pi
- ESP8266 Wi-Fi module (MQTT device)
- CoAP-compatible sensor (e.g., a simple Python script)

Step-by-Step Instructions:
a. Set Up the MQTT Device

- Program the ESP8266 to publish temperature data to an MQTT broker.

```cpp
#include <ESP8266WiFi.h>
#include <PubSubClient.h>
#include <DHT.h>
#define DHTPIN 2
#define DHTTYPE DHT11
DHT dht(DHTPIN, DHTTYPE);
const char* ssid = "your_SSID";
const char* password = "your_PASSWORD";
const char* mqttServer = "broker.hivemq.com";
const int mqttPort = 1883;
const char* mqttTopic = "iot/temperature";
WiFiClient espClient;
PubSubClient client(espClient);
void setup() {
Serial.begin(115200);
dht.begin();
WiFi.begin(ssid, password);
while (WiFi.status() != WL_CONNECTED) {
delay(500);
Serial.print(".");
}
Serial.println("WiFi connected");
client.setServer(mqttServer, mqttPort);
client.connect("ESP8266Client");
}
void loop() {
float temperature = dht.readTemperature();
if (!isnan(temperature)) {
client.publish(mqttTopic, String(temperature).c_str());
}
delay(2000);
}
```

b. Set Up the CoAP Device

- Create a simple CoAP server using a Python script on another device or the Raspberry Pi.

```python
from coapthon.server.coap import CoAP
from coapthon.resources.resource import Resource
import logging
class TemperatureResource(Resource):
def __init__(self, name="TemperatureResource"):
super(TemperatureResource, self).__init__(name)
self.payload = "Temperature: 0.0"
def render_GET(self, request):
return self
def render_PUT(self, request):
self.payload = request.payload
return self
class CoAPServer(CoAP):
def __init__(self, host, port):
CoAP.__init__(self, (host, port))
self.add_resource('temperature/', TemperatureResource())
logging.basicConfig(level=logging.INFO)
server = CoAPServer("0.0.0.0", 5683)
try:
server.listen(10)
except KeyboardInterrupt:
server.close()
```

c. Create the Bridge on Raspberry Pi

- Use a Python script on the Raspberry Pi to bridge MQTT and CoAP.

```python
import paho.mqtt.client as mqtt
import requests
MQTT_BROKER = "broker.hivemq.com"
MQTT_TOPIC = "iot/temperature"
COAP_URL = "coap://localhost:5683/temperature"
def on_message(client, userdata, message):
temperature = message.payload.decode("utf-8")
requests.put(COAP_URL, data=temperature)
mqtt_client = mqtt.Client()
mqtt_client.on_message = on_message
mqtt_client.connect(MQTT_BROKER)
mqtt_client.subscribe(MQTT_TOPIC)
mqtt_client.loop_start()
try:
while True:
pass
except KeyboardInterrupt:
mqtt_client.loop_stop()
mqtt_client.disconnect()
```

Summary

In this chapter, we explored advanced IoT concepts, including edge computing, machine learning in IoT, and IoT interoperability. We discussed their benefits, use cases, and provided practical examples to demonstrate their implementation. Understanding these advanced topics will help you design more sophisticated and efficient IoT systems.

Keep Going!

You're making great progress in your journey to understand IoT systems! In the next chapter, we will discuss tips and best practices for designing and implementing IoT systems effectively. Let's move on and learn how to optimize your IoT projects!

Chapter 9: Tips and Best Practices
Introduction

Designing and implementing IoT systems can be complex and challenging. To help you succeed, this chapter provides valuable tips and best practices for creating efficient, reliable, and secure IoT solutions. We will cover various aspects of IoT development, including hardware design, software development, data management, and security.

Efficient Hardware Design

1. Choose the Right Components

- Select sensors, actuators, and development boards that meet your project's requirements for performance, power consumption, and cost.

- Consider the operating environment and durability of the components.

2. Optimize Power Consumption

- Use low-power components and design your system to enter low-power modes when not in use.

- Consider energy harvesting techniques (e.g., solar power) for battery-operated devices.

3. Ensure Reliable Connectivity

- Choose appropriate communication protocols and technologies based on your project's range, bandwidth, and power requirements.

- Implement redundancy and failover mechanisms to maintain connectivity in case of network issues.

4. Plan for Scalability

- Design your hardware to accommodate future expansions, such as adding more sensors or upgrading to more powerful processors.

Robust Software Development

1. Modular Code Design

- Write modular and reusable code to simplify development, debugging, and maintenance.

- Break your code into smaller functions and libraries for better organization.

2. Implement Error Handling

- Include comprehensive error handling and logging to diagnose and fix issues quickly.

- Use try-catch blocks in your code to manage exceptions gracefully.

3. Use Version Control

- Use version control systems (e.g., Git) to track changes, collaborate with others, and manage code versions.

- Commit code changes frequently and write meaningful commit messages.

4. Test Thoroughly

- Conduct thorough testing, including unit tests, integration tests, and end-to-end tests, to ensure your system works as expected.

- Use automated testing tools to streamline the testing process.

5. Optimize Performance

- Optimize your code for performance, especially in resource-constrained devices.

- Profile your code to identify and eliminate bottlenecks.

Effective Data Management

1. Data Collection and Storage

- Collect only the necessary data to reduce storage and processing overhead.

- Use efficient data formats (e.g., JSON, CBOR) and compress data when possible.

2. Data Processing and Analysis

- Process data at the edge when possible to reduce latency and bandwidth usage.

- Use cloud-based analytics services to gain insights from large datasets.

3. Ensure Data Privacy and Security

- Encrypt data both in transit and at rest to protect it from unauthorized access.

- Implement access control mechanisms to restrict data access to authorized users and applications.

4. Comply with Regulations

- Ensure your data management practices comply with relevant regulations (e.g., GDPR, HIPAA) to avoid legal issues.

Implementing Security Best Practices

1. Secure Device Boot

- Implement secure boot mechanisms to ensure that devices boot using only trusted software.

- Use hardware-based security modules (e.g., TPM, secure elements) for added protection.

2. Strong Authentication

- Use strong authentication mechanisms, such as mutual TLS, to verify device identity before allowing network access.

- Regularly rotate keys and certificates to minimize the risk of compromised credentials.

3. Data Encryption

- Encrypt data at rest and in transit using strong encryption algorithms (e.g., AES-256, RSA).

- Use secure communication protocols (e.g., HTTPS, MQTT over TLS) to protect data during transmission.

4. Regular Firmware Updates

- Implement over-the-air (OTA) updates to keep device firmware up-to-date with the latest security patches.

- Verify the integrity of firmware updates before applying them.

5. Monitor and Audit

- Continuously monitor your IoT system for suspicious activity and potential security threats.

- Implement logging and auditing mechanisms to track access and changes to your system.

6. Educate Users

- Educate users on best practices for securing their IoT devices and networks.

- Provide clear instructions on configuring and maintaining device security settings.

Practical Example: Implementing OTA Updates on ESP32

Let's implement a simple OTA update mechanism for an ESP32 device to demonstrate how to keep device firmware up-to-date.

Components Needed:

- ESP32 development board
- Arduino IDE

Step-by-Step Instructions:

1. Install Required Libraries

- Install the "ArduinoOTA" library in the Arduino IDE.

2. Write the Arduino Code

```cpp
#include <WiFi.h>
#include <ArduinoOTA.h>
const char* ssid = "your_SSID";
const char* password = "your_PASSWORD";
void setup() {
Serial.begin(115200);
WiFi.begin(ssid, password);
while (WiFi.status() != WL_CONNECTED) {
delay(500);
Serial.print(".");
}
Serial.println("WiFi connected");
// Initialize OTA
ArduinoOTA.onStart([]() {
String type;
if (ArduinoOTA.getCommand() == U_FLASH) {
type = "sketch";
} else {
type = "filesystem";
}
Serial.println("Start updating " + type);
});
ArduinoOTA.onEnd([]() {
Serial.println("\nEnd");
});
ArduinoOTA.onProgress([](unsigned int progress, unsigned int
total) {
Serial.printf("Progress: %u%%\r", (progress / (total / 100)));
});
ArduinoOTA.onError([](ota_error_t error) {
Serial.printf("Error[%u]: ", error);
if (error == OTA_AUTH_ERROR) {
```

```
Serial.println("Auth Failed");
} else if (error == OTA_BEGIN_ERROR) {
Serial.println("Begin Failed");
} else if (error == OTA_CONNECT_ERROR) {
Serial.println("Connect Failed");
} else if (error == OTA_RECEIVE_ERROR) {
Serial.println("Receive Failed");
} else if (error == OTA_END_ERROR) {
Serial.println("End Failed");
}
});
ArduinoOTA.begin();
}
void loop() {
ArduinoOTA.handle();
}
```

3. Upload the Initial Code

- Upload the initial code to the ESP32 using a USB connection.

4. Perform OTA Update

- Modify the code (e.g., change the Serial.println("WiFi connected"); message) and upload it over the air.

- In the Arduino IDE, select the network port corresponding to the ESP32 and click "Upload."

Summary

In this chapter, we explored tips and best practices for designing and implementing IoT systems. We covered efficient hardware design, robust software development, effective data management, and security best practices. Implementing these recommendations will help you create efficient, reliable, and secure IoT solutions.

Keep Going!

You're making great progress in your journey to understand IoT systems! In the next chapter, we will explore resources and further reading to help you continue learning and expanding your knowledge in IoT. Let's move on and discover additional learning opportunities!

Chapter 10: Resources and Further Reading

Introduction

Continuing your education and staying updated with the latest developments in IoT is crucial for mastering this rapidly evolving field. In this chapter, we will explore various resources for further learning, including books, online courses, software tools, websites, and forums. These resources will help you deepen your understanding of IoT and keep up with emerging technologies and best practices.

Recommended Books and Publications

1. "Internet of Things: A Hands-On Approach" by Arshdeep Bahga and Vijay Madisetti

- This book provides a comprehensive introduction to IoT, including detailed explanations of IoT architecture, protocols, and applications. It includes hands-on projects and examples.

2. "Building the Internet of Things: Implement New Business Models, Disrupt Competitors, Transform Your Industry" by Maciej Kranz

- This book explores the business and strategic aspects of IoT, offering insights into how IoT can transform industries and create new business opportunities.

3. **"IoT Fundamentals: Networking Technologies, Protocols, and Use Cases for the Internet of Things" by David Hanes, Gonzalo Salgueiro, Patrick Grossetete, Rob Barton, and Jerome Henry**

- A detailed guide covering the fundamental technologies and protocols used in IoT, along with practical use cases and examples.

4. **"Mastering Internet of Things: Design and create your own IoT applications using Raspberry Pi 3" by Peter Waher**

- Focuses on creating IoT applications with Raspberry Pi, providing practical guidance and projects.

Online Courses and Tutorials

1. Coursera

- **"Introduction to the Internet of Things and Embedded Systems" by University of California, Irvine**: A beginner-friendly course covering the basics of IoT and embedded systems.

- **"IoT: Wireless Communications for IoT" by Yonsei University**: Focuses on wireless communication technologies for IoT applications.

2. edX

- **"IoT Programming and Big Data" by Curtin University**: Teaches programming for IoT devices and handling big data generated by IoT systems.

• **"Introduction to Embedded Systems with ARM"** by **University of Texas at Austin**: Covers the fundamentals of embedded systems and programming with ARM processors.

3. Udacity

• **"IoT Nanodegree Program"**: A comprehensive program that includes building projects with IoT devices, learning about sensors, and developing applications.

4. LinkedIn Learning

• **"IoT Foundations: Fundamentals"**: An introductory course covering the basics of IoT, including hardware, software, and communication protocols.

• **"IoT Foundations: Standards and Ecosystems"**: Explores the standards and ecosystems in the IoT landscape.

Software Tools and Libraries

1. Arduino IDE

• An integrated development environment for writing, compiling, and uploading code to Arduino boards. It supports a wide range of libraries for IoT projects.

2. PlatformIO

• An open-source ecosystem for IoT development that supports multiple development boards and frameworks, including Arduino, ESP8266, ESP32, and more.

3. MQTT.fx

- A desktop application for testing and debugging MQTT connections. It allows you to publish and subscribe to MQTT topics.

4. Node-RED

- A flow-based development tool for visual programming, suitable for wiring together hardware devices, APIs, and online services.

5. ThingSpeak

- An IoT analytics platform that enables you to collect, visualize, and analyze data from IoT devices.

6. InfluxDB

- A time-series database designed for high-performance data ingestion and querying, ideal for storing IoT data.

Websites and Forums

1. Stack Overflow

- A community-driven Q&A platform where you can ask questions and find answers related to IoT development, programming, and troubleshooting.

2. Arduino Forum

- A forum dedicated to Arduino users, where you can find discussions, tutorials, and help for your Arduino-based IoT projects.

3. Reddit

- **r/IOT**: A subreddit dedicated to IoT discussions, news, projects, and questions.

- **r/arduino**: A subreddit focused on Arduino projects, tutorials, and support.

4. Hackster.io

- A community for hardware developers where you can find projects, tutorials, and resources for IoT development.

5. Adafruit Learning System

- Offers tutorials, guides, and projects for a wide range of IoT-related topics and hardware.

Technical Documentation

1. Arduino Documentation

- Official documentation for Arduino boards, libraries, and examples.

2. Microcontroller Datasheets

- Datasheets for microcontrollers and other components used in IoT projects, available from manufacturers' websites.

3. Software User Manuals

- User manuals for software tools like MATLAB, LabVIEW, and Python libraries, providing detailed instructions and examples.

Communities

1. IEEE IoT

- A professional organization that provides resources, publications, and conferences related to IoT.

2. Online Communities

- Platforms like LinkedIn, Reddit, and specialized forums where professionals and enthusiasts discuss IoT topics and share knowledge.

3. Meetup Groups

- Local meetup groups focused on IoT, where you can network, attend workshops, and collaborate on projects.

Summary

In this chapter, we explored various resources for further learning and staying updated with the latest developments in IoT. These resources include recommended books, online courses, software tools, websites, forums, technical documentation, and professional communities. Leveraging these resources will help you deepen your understanding of IoT and keep up with emerging technologies and best practices.

Chapter 11: Conclusion and Next Steps

Summary of Key Points

Congratulations on reaching the end of "The Essential Guide to IoT: Building Smart Systems with Arduino and Beyond." Let's recap some of the key points covered throughout the book:

1. **Introduction to IoT**: We started with an overview of IoT, its history, key components, and various applications. We discussed the difference between sensors and actuators, and how they interact within IoT systems.
2. **IoT Architecture**: We explored the architecture of IoT systems, including the perception layer, connectivity layer, edge computing layer, data processing layer, and application layer. Understanding this layered approach is crucial for designing scalable and efficient IoT solutions.
3. **Hardware for IoT**: We delved into the hardware components used in IoT projects, including popular development boards (Arduino, Raspberry Pi, ESP8266, ESP32), sensors, and actuators. Practical examples demonstrated how to interface these components with development boards.
4. **Communication Protocols**: We covered various communication protocols used in IoT, such as MQTT, CoAP, HTTP, and WebSockets, and discussed different connectivity options like Wi-Fi, Bluetooth, Zigbee, LoRa, and cellular networks. Practical examples illustrated how to implement these protocols in IoT projects.
5. **Data Acquisition and Processing**: We discussed techniques for collecting, processing, and storing data from IoT devices, including local data processing on edge devices and cloud-

based storage and analytics services. Practical examples showed how to send data to cloud platforms like AWS IoT.

6. **Cloud Platforms for IoT**: We explored popular IoT cloud platforms (AWS IoT, Azure IoT, Google Cloud IoT), their key features, and how to set up IoT devices on these platforms. Practical examples demonstrated data transmission and monitoring on these platforms.

7. **Security in IoT**: We emphasized the importance of security in IoT systems and discussed best practices for securing IoT devices, including secure boot, device authentication, data encryption, regular firmware updates, and network security.

8. **Advanced IoT Concepts**: We covered advanced topics such as edge computing, machine learning in IoT, and IoT interoperability. Practical examples demonstrated how to implement edge computing and anomaly detection in IoT projects.

9. **Tips and Best Practices**: We provided valuable tips and best practices for designing and implementing IoT systems, including efficient hardware design, robust software development, effective data management, and security best practices.

10. **Resources and Further Reading**: We listed various resources for further learning, including recommended books, online courses, software tools, websites, forums, technical documentation, and professional communities.

Final Thoughts

IoT is a transformative technology that extends the power of the internet to a vast array of devices, enabling smarter interactions with the physical world. By understanding the fundamental principles and practical applications of IoT, you have gained valuable skills that can be applied to real-world projects. The journey of learning and exploring IoT is ongoing, and the opportunities are endless.

Next Steps

Here are some suggestions for your next steps in mastering IoT:

1. **Continue Learning**: Use the resources provided in the previous chapter to deepen your knowledge. Explore advanced topics, take online courses, and read more books on IoT.

2. **Hands-On Projects**: Apply what you've learned by working on hands-on projects. Experiment with different sensors, actuators, and communication protocols. Try building more complex IoT systems and refine your skills through practice.

3. **Join Communities**: Engage with professional communities and forums. Share your projects, ask questions, and learn from others. Networking with fellow enthusiasts and professionals can provide valuable insights and support.

4. **Attend Conferences and Workshops**: Participate in conferences and workshops related to IoT. These events offer opportunities to learn about the latest developments, present your work, and connect with experts in the field.

5. **Stay Updated**: Keep yourself updated with the latest advancements in IoT. Subscribe to journals, follow relevant blogs and websites, and stay informed about new technologies and trends.

6. **Collaborate and Innovate**: Collaborate with others on projects and research. Innovation often comes from teamwork and the exchange of ideas. Work with peers, join research groups, and contribute to open-source projects.

Conclusion

You have embarked on an exciting journey to understand and master IoT. This book has provided you with a solid foundation and practical skills to design and implement IoT systems using Arduino and beyond. As you continue to explore and grow in this field, remember to stay curious, keep experimenting, and never stop learning.

Thank you for choosing "The Essential Guide to IoT: Building Smart Systems with Arduino and Beyond." We wish you the best of luck in your future endeavors and hope this book has inspired you to continue exploring the fascinating world of IoT.

Keep Innovating!

You've completed the journey through this book, but your adventure with IoT has just begun. Use the knowledge and skills you've gained to create, innovate, and make a difference in the world of technology. The possibilities are endless, and your journey is just beginning!

Appendices

Appendix A: Glossary of Terms A comprehensive glossary of key terms and concepts discussed in the book.

Appendix B: Useful IoT Libraries and Tools A list of useful libraries and tools for IoT development, organized by category.

Appendix C: Additional Resources for Learning IoT A curated list of additional resources, including books, courses, websites, and forums, for continued learning and exploration in IoT.

Appendix A: Glossary of Terms

Actuator: A device that converts an electrical signal into physical action, such as a motor or a relay.

Analog Sensor: A sensor that produces a continuous signal proportional to the physical quantity being measured, such as temperature or light intensity.

Arduino: An open-source electronics platform based on easy-to-use hardware and software, commonly used for prototyping and building IoT projects.

Bluetooth: A short-range wireless communication technology used for exchanging data between devices over short distances.

CoAP (Constrained Application Protocol): A specialized web transfer protocol designed for use with constrained nodes and networks in the IoT.

Cloud Computing: The delivery of computing services (such as storage, processing, and analytics) over the internet, allowing for scalable and flexible resource management.

DHT11/DHT22: Common temperature and humidity sensors used in IoT projects.

Edge Computing: A distributed computing paradigm that processes data near the source of data generation (i.e., at the edge of the network) rather than in a centralized cloud.

ESP8266/ESP32: Low-cost Wi-Fi microcontrollers with full TCP/IP stack and microcontroller capability, popular in IoT projects.

HTTP (Hypertext Transfer Protocol): A widely used protocol for transmitting hypermedia documents, such as HTML, and commonly used for web-based IoT applications.

IoT (Internet of Things): A network of interconnected physical devices embedded with sensors, software, and other technologies to collect and exchange data over the internet.

JSON (JavaScript Object Notation): A lightweight data interchange format that is easy for humans to read and write and easy for machines to parse and generate.

LoRa (Long Range): A low-power, long-range wireless communication technology used for wide-area networks in IoT.

MQTT (Message Queuing Telemetry Transport): A lightweight, publish-subscribe network protocol that transports messages between devices in IoT applications.

Node-RED: A flow-based development tool for visual programming, suitable for wiring together hardware devices, APIs, and online services.

PID Control: A control loop feedback mechanism (Proportional-Integral-Derivative) commonly used in industrial control systems.

Pub/Sub (Publish/Subscribe): A messaging pattern where senders (publishers) send messages to a topic, and receivers (subscribers) receive messages from the topic.

Raspberry Pi: A small, affordable computer that can be used for a wide range of IoT projects, often running a full operating system.

Sensor: A device that detects and measures physical properties from the environment and converts them into signals for processing.

TLS/SSL (Transport Layer Security/Secure Sockets Layer): Cryptographic protocols designed to provide secure communication over a computer network.

Wi-Fi: A wireless networking technology that allows devices to communicate without direct cable connections, commonly used in IoT for high data rate and wide availability.

Zigbee: A wireless mesh protocol for low-power, low-data-rate communication, often used in home automation and industrial control.

Appendix B: Useful IoT Libraries and Tools

Arduino Libraries

- **DHT:** Library for reading temperature and humidity from DHT sensors.
- **ESP8266WiFi:** Library for connecting to Wi-Fi networks with ESP8266.
- **PubSubClient:** MQTT client library for Arduino.
- **ArduinoOTA:** Library for over-the-air updates for ESP8266 and ESP32.

Python Libraries

- **Adafruit_DHT:** Library for reading data from DHT sensors.

- **paho-mqtt:** MQTT client library for Python.

- **requests:** Library for making HTTP requests in Python.

- **scikit-learn:** Machine learning library for Python, useful for data analysis and anomaly detection.

Development Tools

- **Arduino IDE:** Integrated development environment for writing, compiling, and uploading code to Arduino boards.

- PlatformIO: Open-source ecosystem for IoT development, supporting multiple development boards and frameworks.

- MQTT.fx: Desktop application for testing and debugging MQTT connections.

- Node-RED: Flow-based development tool for visual programming of IoT applications.

Cloud Platforms

- AWS IoT Core: Managed cloud service for connecting IoT devices and processing IoT data.

- Azure IoT Hub: Centralized service for bi-directional communication between IoT applications and devices.

- Google Cloud IoT Core: Managed service for secure device connection and management, integrated with other Google Cloud services.

Time-Series Databases

- InfluxDB: Time-series database designed for high-performance data ingestion and querying, ideal for storing IoT data.

- Amazon Timestream: Fully managed time-series database service by AWS.

Appendix C: Additional Resources for Learning IoT

Books

- "Internet of Things: A Hands-On Approach" by Arshdeep Bahga and Vijay Madisetti

- "Building the Internet of Things" by Maciej Kranz

- "IoT Fundamentals" by David Hanes et al.

- "Mastering Internet of Things" by Peter Waher

Online Courses

- Coursera: "Introduction to the Internet of Things and Embedded Systems" by University of California, Irvine

- edX: "IoT Programming and Big Data" by Curtin University

- Udacity: "IoT Nanodegree Program"

- LinkedIn Learning: "IoT Foundations: Fundamentals"

Websites and Forums

- Stack Overflow: Q&A platform for IoT development, programming, and troubleshooting.

- Arduino Forum: Discussions, tutorials, and help for Arduino-based IoT projects.

- **Reddit:** Subreddits like r/IOT and r/arduino for discussions and support.

- **Hackster.io:** Community for hardware developers with projects, tutorials, and resources.

- **Adafruit Learning System:** Tutorials, guides, and projects for IoT-related topics and hardware.

Professional Communities and Conferences

- **IEEE IoT:** Resources, publications, and conferences related to IoT.

- **IoT World:** Annual conference for IoT professionals.

- **Meetup Groups:** Local meetup groups focused on IoT for networking, workshops, and collaboration.